Scientific Concepts Through Models and Analogies

Victoria Stutt, Author

Dr Andrew Chandler-Grevatt, Series Editor

About the author

Victoria Stutt is an experienced science teacher, having taught at KS3, GCSE and post-16. Victoria has written and co-authored many science titles, including KS3 Homework Tasks and teacher materials to cover new specifications, GCSE Chemistry Tasks and A-Level transition material and text books.

About the editor

Dr Andrew Chandler-Grevatt is an experienced Advanced Skills Teacher who now works at the University of Sussex as a Science Education Teaching Fellow. He is the author of the bestselling Level Ladders published by Badger Learning.

Badger Learning
Suite G08
Business & Technology Centre
Bessemer Drive
Stevenage, Hertfordshire
SG1 2DX

Telephone: 01438 791037
Fax: 01438 791036
www.badgerlearning.co.uk
info@badgerlearning.co.uk

Scientific Concepts Through Models and Analogies
Victoria Stutt
First published 2014
ISBN 978-1-78464-052-1

Text © Victoria Stutt 2014
Illustrations © Juliet Breese 2014
Complete work © Badger Publishing

Publisher: Susan Ross
Author: Victoria Stutt
Series Editor: Dr Andrew Chandler-Grevatt
Project Editor: Ursula Faulkner
Illustrations: Juliet Breese
Text and Cover Design: Jo Digby Designs

Printed in the UK

PREFACE

In my work I often see trainee teachers using analogies to help explain abstract or complex scientific concepts to their students. Sometimes these are planned ahead, sometimes in the midst of questioning, the teacher will spontaneously come up with an analogy. Teachers, particularly science teachers, use analogies to help develop the understanding of their students.

As I have researched the use of analogies, models and modelling, it is clear that good teachers choose analogies carefully, being aware of their strengths and limitations. However, it is excellent teachers who engage their students with the analogies, supporting them to critique the analogy and strengthen their understanding of the target scientific concept. Further to that, encouraging students to develop their own analogies of scientific concepts has huge benefits for both the teacher and learner. Not only does it give the student ownership of their learning, it gives teachers an opportunity to assess the students' understanding and intervene.

I have had great pleasure in editing these exciting, engaging and educational tasks. This book contains a rich resource that encourages students to engage critically with analogies of difficult scientific concepts and to create their own improved or original versions. I can see these being a useful addition to any scheme of work as starters, whole lessons or engaging homework activities.

Dr Andy Chandler-Grevatt
Series Editor

CONTENTS

INTRODUCTION

Why should I use analogies and models in my science teaching?

Much of the science we teach cannot be seen, it is abstract. In order to understand it, most students need to be able to visualise it. If we use a familiar scenario that can be seen or experienced, this can give a starting point, on which students can build their new knowledge. Using real life situations can also motivate some students.

'Teaching with analogies can be fun and motivating for students, and research suggests it also enhances student learning of scientific concepts' *Using Analogies in Middle and Secondary Science Classrooms: the FAR Guide – An Interesting Way to Teach with Analogies,* edited by Harrison and Coll, Corwin Press, 2008, California

Learning scientific concepts is not a passive process, students must construct their own ideas and knowledge, and through using models and analogies they can do this. Each student will visualise the model or analogy differently and so will have to make their own choices about how the model is similar to, or different from, the concept being considered. Models are not perfect and will all contain flaws. It is through identifying and considering these flaws that students' learning is embedded.

What is included with each task?

Each task contains

- **Teacher's Notes** This includes the National Curriculum link(s) and an **ACE Learning Ladder** to be used as broad guidance on the understanding being demonstrated by students. Detailed guidance on how to use ACE Learning Ladders is provided below.
- **Stimulus Sheet** that should be given to, or displayed for, students. The stimulus sheet is presented in a very open-ended way, so that students can have freedom to consider the model or analogy in their own way.
- **Discussion Starters** These are optional suggested sentence starters to help students consider how the model or analogy may represent the concept. If required these could be printed out and given to students. The Word document on the CD allows teachers to edit the Discussion Starters, so questions can be removed or added, to suit the needs of given students or classes.

How should I use the tasks?

Students will need to have met the relevant topics the tasks relate to before using the tasks. The tasks are intended to be used as a qualitative summative assessment task, or as a stimulus for discussion on topics already covered in lessons. The tasks can be used to gauge the level of understanding of a topic students have achieved, or to help identify any misconceptions that have arisen.

The tasks would be ideal for use as starter, main or plenary activities or homework part way into a topic. One suggested approach to using the tasks is as follows: depending on the time available, the student sheet (the Stimulus Sheet) should be displayed, for example, as printed sheets or via an interactive screen. Students should be given adequate time to consider the model or analogy, before discussing the concept in question. This discussion can take place in small groups or as a class. The initial consideration of the model should be student led, with students being encouraged to correct or extend the answers of each other. The second stage of discussions should then be teacher led, with open-ended and guiding questions (for example, 'But what would happen if… ?', 'Wouldn't that mean that… ?', 'How is that similar to… ?') being used to help counter misconceptions that may have been apparent. The discussions do not need to be formally split into two parts, there should be a natural flow, but it is important not to jump in and give the 'answers' before students have had a chance to consider the model and work collaboratively to pick the model or analogy apart.

To promote discussions about the model, questions could be displayed on an interactive whiteboard or as flash cards. The level of questions should be adapted to the age and ability of your students. The goal is for students to be able to consider their own *student model* (i.e. their interpretation of the analogy or model shown) against the *target model* (i.e. what actually happens; the scientific concept), and move their understanding towards the target model.

After the model has been fully discussed, it is beneficial to provide an opportunity to consolidate the points within the model. In order to do this, you may wish to provide questions to answer, or ask students to act out an improved model, or produce an A3 cartoon of their own depicting an improved model, or indeed a brand new model. Students should provide written information or give verbal discussions of how their models or analogies represent the concepts. Following the activity, the comments and thoughts of students will have given a good indication of current understanding of topics. This should then inform the planning of subsequent lessons.

It is essential to note that the models and analogies shown will have inherent flaws (as all models do), students who are *confident* or *advanced* must be encouraged to rectify these, students who are *establishing* would not be expected to rectify flaws but should be able to begin spotting simple problems in the model or analogy.

The tasks are broken down into the three main subject areas, biology, chemistry and physics. They are not intended to be worked through one at a time, but rather to be dipped in and out of as they are relevant. The best time to use them will depend heavily on the particular class, high-ability classes may be ready to consider models very early on, whereas with low-ability classes, it would be better to wait until later in a topic so that basic understanding is secure.

A final note – there are numerous discussions over what constitutes a model and an analogy. For the purposes of this book, I have chosen a fairly arbitrary classification: anything that can be physically demonstrated, for example with simple apparatus, I have called a model; anything that requires the student to imagine a scenario, I have called an analogy.

How can I use ACE Learning Ladders to gauge student performance?

We have introduced the ACE Learning Ladder, which can be used in a variety of ways to suit the needs or assessment system of your school.

A is for Advanced

The descriptors at this stage relate to the old Level 7 and 8 or an equivalent to grade A. They indicate that the student is working beyond expectation of the National Curriculum for Key Stage 3.

C is for Confident

The descriptors at this stage relate to the old Level 5 and 6 or an equivalent to grade C. They indicate that the student is working at the expectation of the National Curriculum for Key Stage 3. From a 'mastery' perspective, students working at this stage have mastered this KS3 knowledge, understanding or skills within the programme of study.

E is for Establishing

The descriptors at this stage relate to the old Level 3 and 4 or an equivalent to grade E. They indicate that the student is currently working below the expectation of the National Curriculum for Key Stage 3. Students working at this stage will need support and intervention to become confident.

Encouragement of the use of ACE Learning Ladders

Some learners find it difficult to use the ACE Learning Ladder to guide their work. Strategies we have seen used include:

- encouraging the learner to tick or highlight the statements on the ACE Learning Ladder when they think they have satisfied it
- use an exemplar and show the students how to mark it using the ACE Learning Ladder.

Predominantly, I would expect that these tasks suit teacher assessment, although peer feedback should form a pivotal part during consideration of the models and analogies.

Teacher assessment

If you have not used these tasks before, we would recommend starting with the teacher assessment approach for assessing the learners' responses to the tasks. These are not like the standard tests or exams, where you have very clear guidance of what answers to accept and not accept. This approach is much more flexible and requires the use of professional judgement when assigning a level.

These tasks are not summative tests, so the level that is assigned to a learner's work is only a 'snapshot'. Learners often vary in their achievement from topic to topic. A good analogy to use with them is that of computer games. Computer games are often based on stages of success. Some people score more highly on some computer games than others. The same will be experienced when doing the tasks. However, most learners show a general improvement trend when using these tasks.

The ACE Learning Ladders are written in learner-friendly language. These should be used when communicating achievement and progress with a learner. Additional guidance is given for teachers in the teacher notes – this should be used alongside the ACE Learning Ladder.

As with all new approaches, learners may need to do a few of these tasks before they get the full benefit from them. The tasks are very open, and to start with, some learners can feel overwhelmed by the freedom. They may need a lot of support and encouragement for the first few, as their confidence grows the learners gain more independence at attempting the tasks.

Do not get too bogged down in which grade to assign – make a judgement using the criteria, then assign the grade. We find that learners do pick up on anything they think has been badly judged! The resulting discussion is very useful to both parties.

Self-assessment and peer-assessment

Encouraging learners to assess their own work, or each others', can be very valuable. As with anything new, learners will need more guidance and support to start with before their confidence develops to do this successfully. We would highly recommend that time is taken to help learners develop these skills with the support of these tasks.

Self-assessment can be done by guiding learners through the ACE Learning Ladder and encouraging them to tick off the descriptors they feel they have satisfied. Then, they can use the ACE Learning Ladder to help decide on suitable improvement targets. Peer assessment can be useful because learners can learn from each other as well as engage with what is required for each grade.

Generally, learners are reasonably accurate at assigning grades, but when self-assessing they may not be aware of misconceptions they have made. If you intend the learners to self-assess a piece of work in class, it is worth making sure that you challenge major misconceptions as you circulate.

NATIONAL CURRICULUM LINK

CELLS AND ORGANISATION

- the hierarchical organisation of multicellular organisms: from cells to tissues to organs to systems to organisms

GUIDANCE ON THE ANALOGY

Student interpretation of the analogy can vary and still be correct. However, as a general guide, the individual police officers are representing individual cells. When they work together to carry out the same role this is representing tissues. When the units work together within a police force this is representing various tissues working together as an organ. When various police forces work together as the UK Police, this represents an organ system. The organism could be discussed as being similar to all the international police forces working together. Students should identify flaws in the analogy. For example, there not being the same number of organisation levels as within the body (which is five); the police officers are all the same in terms of their structure (ignoring differences in appearances and characteristics) whereas cells can have completely different structures to suit their roles (e.g. nerve cells and red blood cells); and the police officers within a unit may have slightly different roles, or attend different jobs, whereas all the cells in a tissue carry out the same function.

Please refer to the generic guidance on pp 7–8 on how to use the following ACE Learning Ladder.

ACE LEARNING LADDER

Performance	Students may:
Advanced	• Explain in detail how the police force analogy explains the hierarchical organisation of cells. • Explain the limitations of the police force analogy compared to the actual hierarchical organisation of cells. • Explain how the analogy could be improved or suggest and explain your own model for hierarchical organisation of cells.
Confident	• Describe how the police force analogy represents the hierarchical organisation of cells. • Describe the differences between the police force analogy and the actual hierarchical organisation of cells. • Describe how the analogy could be improved.
Establishing	• Match the parts of the police force analogy to the key parts of the hierarchical organisation of cells. • State one problem with the analogy. • State how the analogy can be improved.

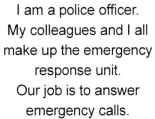

I am a police officer. My colleagues and I all make up the emergency response unit. Our job is to answer emergency calls.

I am a police officer too. My colleagues and I all work on the dog unit. We use dogs to find people and property.

All our units work together for Southtown Police Force. We protect the people of Southtown.

I am a police officer too. My colleagues and I work for the investigation unit as detectives. Our job is to solve serious crimes.

Southtown Police Force work alongside all the other Police Forces in the UK to protect the country. I think that all together we are like cells in the body. What do you think?

POSSIBLE KEYWORDS TO USE:

cell, different, level, organ, organ system, organisation, role, similar, tissue

What does the analogy describe or explain?

- I think each police officer would represent…

- I think the special units (e.g. the dog unit) represent…

- All the police officers in each unit do the same job, this is important because…

- I think Southtown Police Force could represent…

- I think all the UK Police Forces together could represent…

What are the limitations of the analogy?

- The analogy has four levels of organisation. This is/is not the same as in the body because…

- Using police officers as an analogy to explain how cells are arranged in the body is good because…

- Using police officers as an analogy to explain how cells are arranged in the body is not good because…

How could the analogy be improved?

- The analogy could be improved by…

- I would adapt the analogy by …

- A better analogy would be…

- I would improve the analogy by…

BIOLOGY 2: TEACHER'S NOTES
SUBSTANCES MOVING IN AND OUT OF CELLS

NATIONAL CURRICULUM LINK

CELLS AND ORGANISATION

- the role of diffusion in the movement of materials in and between cells

GUIDANCE ON THE ANALOGY

Student interpretation of the analogy can vary and still be correct. However, as a general guide, the Underground train network would represent the circulatory system and the people using the trains the actual blood. They would be carrying glucose, oxygen, carbon dioxide and water represented by packages they may have with them. The movement from the platform onto the train and vice versa represents diffusion into and out of the cells. Students may go on to suggest that the actual cells and reactions that occur within these would be represented by people reaching their work and doing a job. Students should identify flaws with the analogy. For example, the trains are not always moving, whereas blood is always moving through the blood stream; the same trains would be used always, whereas the blood can move through different types of vessels (veins, arteries, etc.); the people are all different, whereas substances moving in and out of cells are always the same; and the concentration inside and out of the cell must be different in order for diffusion to occur, whereas in the analogy, the concentration of people inside and outside the cell may not be different but people can still choose to move into or out of the cell.

Please refer to the generic guidance on pp 7–8 on how to use the following ACE Learning Ladder.

ACE LEARNING LADDER

Performance	Students may:
Advanced	• Explain in detail how the Underground analogy explains the movement of substances in and out of cells. • Explain the limitations of the Underground analogy compared to the actual movement of substances in and out of cells. • Explain how the analogy could be improved or suggest and explain your own analogy for the movement of substances in and out of cells.
Confident	• Describe how the Underground analogy represents the movement of substances in and out of cells. • Describe the differences between the Underground analogy and the actual movement of substances in and out of cells. • Describe how the analogy could be improved.
Establishing	• Match the parts of the Underground analogy to the key parts or processes involved in the movement of substances in and out of cells. • State one problem with the Underground analogy. • State how the analogy can be improved

Every day, people use Underground trains to get around London.

People move into the train from the platform and get off the train onto the platform when they reach their destination.

Is the London Underground a good analogy for how substances reach cells and diffuse into and out of cells?

POSSIBLE KEYWORDS TO USE:

carbon dioxide, cell, different, glucose, organ, osmosis, oxygen, remove, respiration, similar, tissue, transport, water

What does the analogy describe or explain?

- I think the train represents…

- I think the people getting on and off the trains would represent…

- I think the different Underground train stations would represent…

- I think the bags and packages people are carrying could represent…

What are the limitations of the analogy?

- There are not always the same number of people on the train and the platform. This is important because…

- People using Underground trains is a good analogy for substances moving in and out of cells because…

- People using Underground trains is not a good analogy for substances moving in and out of cells because…

How could the analogy be improved?

- I would improve the analogy by…

- I think a better analogy for the movement of substances in and out of cells is…

NATIONAL CURRICULUM LINK

GAS EXCHANGE SYSTEMS

- the mechanism of breathing to move air in and out of the lungs, using a pressure model to explain the movement of gases, including simple measurements of lung volume

GUIDANCE ON THE MODEL

Student interpretation of the model can vary and still be correct. However, as a general guide, the glass bell jar represents the chest cavity, the balloons represent the lungs and the rubber covering on the bottom represents the diaphragm. Where possible, students should be shown the bell jar model before using this task. During breathing the diaphragm moves downwards, increasing the volume of the chest and decreasing the pressure in the chest, thus causing air to be drawn into the lungs. This is modelled by the rubber cover being pulled down and the balloons inflating. The opposite occurs when the rubber covering is moved upwards, representing exhaling. Students should notice flaws in the model, such as the bell jar does not move, whereas the ribcage does move during breathing; the diaphragm alone causes the balloons to inflate in the model, whereas the intercostal muscles are involved in the real situation; and there is no gas exchange occurring.

Please refer to the generic guidance on pp 7–8 on how to use the following ACE Learning Ladder.

ACE LEARNING LADDER

Performance	Students may:
Advanced	<ul><li>Explain in detail how the bell jar model explains the workings of the lungs.</li><li>Explain the limitations of the bell jar model compared to the workings of the lungs.</li><li>Explain how the model could be improved or suggest and explain your own model for the workings of the lungs.</li></ul>
Confident	<ul><li>Describe how the bell jar model represents the workings of the lungs.</li><li>Describe the differences between the bell jar model and the actual workings of the lungs.</li><li>Describe how the model could be improved.</li></ul>
Establishing	<ul><li>Match the parts of the bell jar model to the parts involved in the workings of the lungs.</li><li>State one problem with the model.</li><li>State how the model can be improved.</li></ul>

The apparatus shown is called the bell jar model.

Is it a good model for showing what happens during breathing in and breathing out?

POSSIBLE KEYWORDS TO USE:

alveoli, blood, bronchiole, carbon dioxide, capillaries, different, exchange, expand, glass, oxygen, pressure, similar, trachea

What does the model describe or explain?

- I think the tubes represent…

- I think the balloons represent…

- I think the glass bell jar represents…

- I think the rubber cover on the bottom represents…

- I think that when the rubber cover on the bottom is pulled down this represents…

- I think when the rubber cover on the bottom is moved back up this represents…

What are the limitations of the model?

- I think the bell jar model is a good way to model what happens during breathing in because…

- I think the bell jar model is not a good way to model what happens during breathing in because…

- I think the bell jar model is a good way to model what happens during breathing out because…

- I think the bell jar model is not a good way to model what happens during breathing out because…

How could the model be improved?

- I would adapt the model to make it better by…

- I think a better model would be…

BIOLOGY 4: TEACHER'S NOTES
MOVEMENT OF FOOD THROUGH THE INTESTINES

NATIONAL CURRICULUM LINK

NUTRITION AND DIGESTION

- the tissues and organs of the human digestive system, including adaptations to function and how the digestive system digests food (enzymes simply as biological catalysts)

GUIDANCE ON THE MODEL

Student interpretation of the model can vary and still be correct. However, as a general guide, the tube being squeezed represents the intestines and the toothpaste represents the food being passed through. The squeezing action represents the muscles of the gut contracting to push food along. Students should give flaws in the model. For example, the 'food' represented by the toothpaste is all the same, there is no distinction between nutrients being absorbed and fibrous material, for example; toothpaste can only exit at the end of the tube, whereas nutrients are removed from actual food through the walls of the intestines; the squeezing is applied externally to the tube of toothpaste, whereas muscles within the gut wall contract to move food along; and the toothpaste could be squeezed backwards in the tube, whereas food in the gut is squeezed along in the forward direction only.

Please refer to the generic guidance on pp 7–8 on how to use the following ACE Learning Ladder.

BIOLOGY 4: TEACHER'S NOTES
MOVEMENT OF FOOD THROUGH THE INTESTINES

ACE LEARNING LADDER

Performance	Students may:
Advanced	• Explain in detail how the toothpaste tube model explains the movement of food through the intestines. • Explain the limitations of the toothpaste model compared to the actual movement of food through the intestines. • Explain how the model could be improved or suggest and explain your own model for the movement of food through the intestines.
Confident	• Describe how the toothpaste tube model represents the movement of food through the intestines. • Describe the differences between the toothpaste tube model and the movement of food through the intestines. • Describe how the model could be improved.
Establishing	• Match the parts of the toothpaste tube model to the key parts involved in the movement of food through the intestines. • State one problem with the model. • State how the model can be improved.

My toothpaste has nearly run out. I need to squeeze what's left, up from the bottom.

It reminds me of the way food moves through the intestines. Do you agree?

POSSIBLE KEYWORDS TO USE:

absorb, contraction, different, food, intestines, muscle, nutrients, peristalsis, similar, waste

What does the model describe or explain?

- I think the toothpaste in the tube represents…

- I think the plastic tube represents…

- I think the person squeezing the tube represents…

What are the limitations of the model?

- Sometimes the toothpaste only needs to be squeezed once to get some to come out, this is/is not similar to food being moved through the intestines because…

- Toothpaste in the tube would move quickly when squeezed. Food in the intestines would move…

- Toothpaste being squeezed through a tube is a good model for food moving through the intestines because…

- Toothpaste being squeezed through a tube is not a good model for food moving through the intestines because…

How could the model be improved?

- I would improve the model by…

- I think a better model for the movement of food through the intestines is…

1 GETTING NUTRIENTS FROM FOOD

NATIONAL CURRICULUM LINK

NUTRITION AND DIGESTION

- the tissues and organs of the human digestive system, including adaptations to function and how the digestive system digests food (enzymes simply as biological catalysts)

GUIDANCE ON THE MODEL

Student interpretation of the model can vary and still be correct. However, as a general guide, the tights represent the wall of the small intestine. The tin of spaghetti represents food that has been eaten. The tomato sauce passes through the holes in the tights and this represents the useful nutrients being removed from the food and absorbed through the wall of the small intestine and into the bloodstream. The spaghetti that remains represents the undigested food (e.g. fibre) that would continue through the digestive system and be passed as waste. Students should identify flaws with the model. For example, the tights do not contain villi but rather have small holes; the food is merely a mixture that gets separated due to size, whereas food in the intestine is broken down by enzymes before being separated; the spaghetti moves through the tights due to gravity, whereas food in the gut is moved along by peristalsis; and the tomato juice just falls away from the tights, whereas in the intestine blood vessels would surround the small intestine and would absorb the nutrients coming from the food.

Please refer to the generic guidance on pp 7–8 on how to use the following ACE Learning Ladder.

ACE LEARNING LADDER

Performance	Students may:
Advanced	• Explain in detail how the spaghetti and tights model explains how nutrients are obtained from food. • Explain the limitations of the spaghetti and tights model compared to the actual way nutrients are obtained from food. • Explain how the model could be improved or suggest and explain your own model for obtaining nutrients from food.
Confident	• Describe how the spaghetti and tights model represents how nutrients are obtained from food. • Describe the differences between the spaghetti and tights model and the actual way nutrients are obtained from food. • Describe how the model could be improved.
Establishing	• Match the parts of the spaghetti and tights model to the key parts involved in obtaining nutrients from food. • State one problem with the model. • State how the model can be improved.

Would pouring a tin of spaghetti into a pair of tights be a good way to model what happens during digestion?

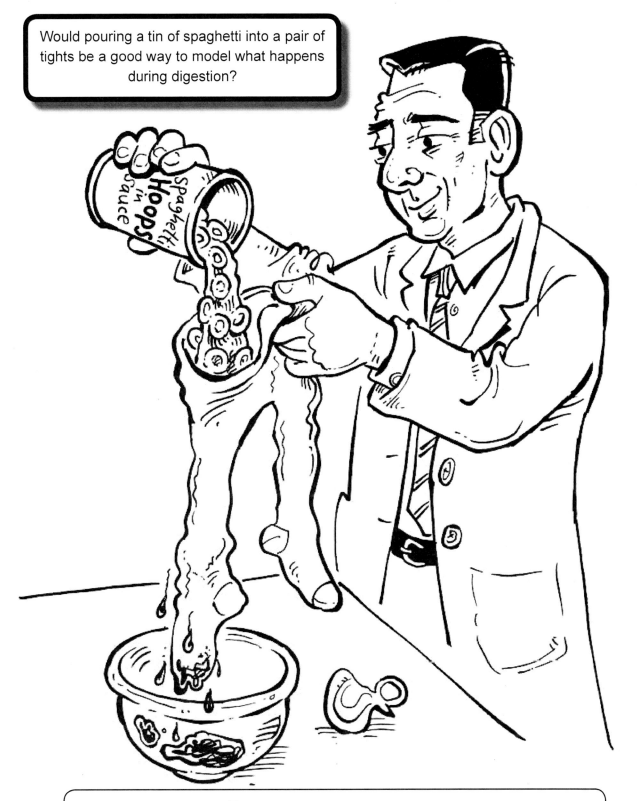

POSSIBLE KEYWORDS TO USE:

absorb, blood, capillary, different, enyzmes, fibre, hole, nutrients, pass, similar, size, villi, waste

What does the model describe or explain?

- I think the tights represent…

- I think the tin of spaghetti represents…

- I think the bits of spaghetti represent…

- I think the tomato sauce represents…

- I think the stage of digestion this model represents is…

What are the limitations of the model?

- This model is similar to what happens during digestion because…

- This model is different to what happens during digestion because…

How could the model be improved?

- I would adapt the model to make it better by…

- I think a better model would be…

NATIONAL CURRICULUM LINK

RELATIONSHIPS IN AN ECOSYSTEM

- the interdependence of organisms in an ecosystem, including food webs and insect pollinated crops

GUIDANCE ON THE ANALOGY

Student interpretation of the analogy can vary and still be correct. However, as a general guide, each person involved in the analogy represents a different organism in a food web. The analogy shows different 'chains' whereby people depend on each other. For example, the restaurant depends on the baker to provide strawberry tarts and the baker in turn relies on the strawberry farmer. These individual chains represent food chains that build up a food web. The products each person is making could be seen to represent energy as it is this that moves through the levels of the web. Predators could be represented by anyone who uses a product made by someone else and, hence, prey could be represented by the person supplying goods. Students should identify flaws in the analogy. For example, the people are not eating each other, unlike in a food web; the first organism in the chain is not a producer as it cannot produce its own energy via photosynthesis; the population changes are seen in the goods made rather than the actual organisms; and not every chain follows the pattern of producer – herbivore – carnivore.

Please refer to the generic guidance on pp 7–8 on how to use the following ACE Learning Ladder.

ACE LEARNING LADDER

Performance	Students may:
Advanced	• Explain in detail how the restaurant analogy explains interdependence in a food web. • Explain the limitations of the restaurant analogy compared to interdependence in a food web. • Explain how the analogy could be improved or suggest and explain your own analogy for interdependence in a food web.
Confident	• Describe how the restaurant analogy represents interdependence in a food web. • Describe the differences between the restaurant analogy and interdependence in a food web. • Describe how the analogy could be improved.
Establishing	• Match the parts of the restaurant analogy to key parts involved in interdependence in a food web. • State one problem with the analogy. • State how the analogy can be improved.

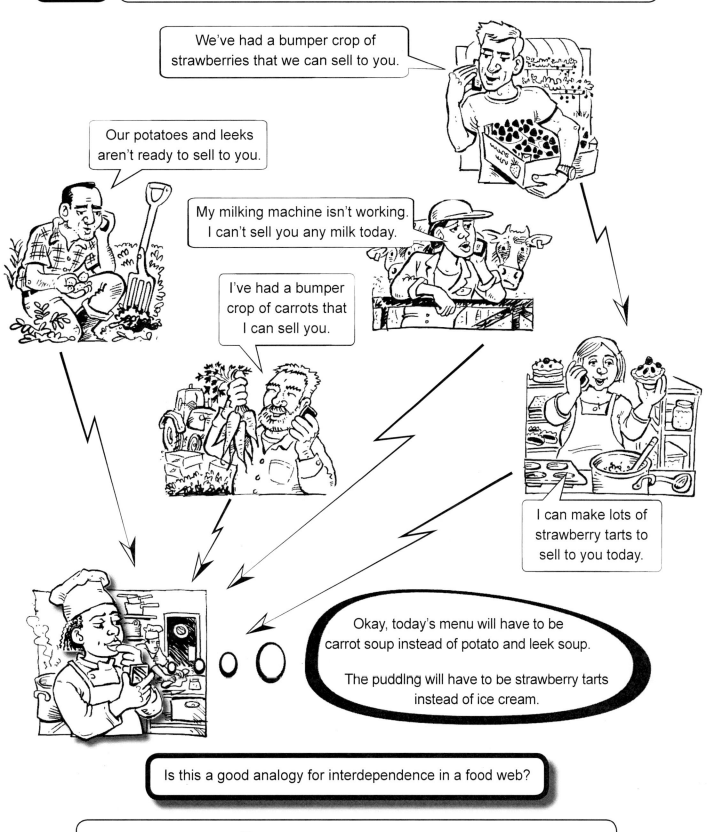

POSSIBLE KEYWORDS TO USE:

consumer, crop, demand, difference, energy, food chain, food web, level,
population, producer, similar, species, supply

What does the analogy describe or explain?

- I think each person in the picture represents…

- Food webs can have different levels. This is represented in the analogy by…

- Food webs show energy transfers. I think this is represented in the analogy by…

What are the limitations of the analogy?

- Organisms in food webs can be producers or consumers. These are/are not represented in the analogy by…

- Organisms can be herbivores or carnivores. This is/is not represented in the analogy because…

- Food webs include predators and prey. This is/is not represented by the analogy because…

- Food webs are made up from lots of food chains. This is shown in the analogy by…

- Changes in food webs cause populations to change. This is/is not shown in the analogy by…

- I think the analogy is a good way of showing interdependence in a food web because…

- I think the analogy is not a good way of showing interdependence in a food web because…

How could the analogy be improved?

- I would adapt the analogy to make it better by…

- I think a better analogy would be…

NATIONAL CURRICULUM LINK

INHERITANCE, CHROMOSOMES, DNA AND GENES

- heredity as the process by which genetic information is transmitted from one generation to the next
- differences between species
- the variation between species and between individuals of the same species means some organisms compete more successfully, which can drive natural selection
- changes in the environment may leave individuals within a species, and some entire species, less well adapted to compete successfully and reproduce, which in turn may lead to extinction

GUIDANCE ON THE ANALOGY

Student interpretation of the analogy can vary and still be correct. However, as a general guide, organisms change over time because they possess genes which make them naturally good at adapting to their environment and these are passed to the next generation more successfully. Useful or effective features in cars will be kept and moved into the next generation of cars, and new features added and so the design of cars evolves over time, with poor features being lost. Students should identify flaws in the analogy. For example, organisms naturally possess certain features, whereas cars have been artificially designed to have given features; the time scale for natural selection is slow, whereas car designs change rapidly; designs are chosen and passed on through design, in living organisms features are passed on through reproduction; and natural selection is unpredictable, whereas artificial design of cars is dictated by the designer who can pick and choose features to keep or change.

Please refer to the generic guidance on pp 7–8 on how to use the following ACE Learning Ladder.

1

ACE LEARNING LADDER

Performance	Students may:
Advanced	• Explain in detail how the car design analogy explains natural selection. • Explain the limitations of the car design analogy compared to natural selection. • Explain how the analogy could be improved or suggest and explain your own analogy for natural selection.
Confident	• Describe how the car design analogy represents natural selection. • Describe the differences between the car design analogy and natural selection. • Describe how the analogy could be improved.
Establishing	• Match the parts of the car design analogy to the processes or things involved in natural selection. • State one problem with the analogy. • State how the analogy can be improved.

Cars have changed a lot since they were first invented. Cars are engineered to suit our changing needs. Living organisms also change through time.

Is the way cars have changed through history a good analogy for natural selection?

Possible keywords to use:

adaptation, choice, design, different, evolution, extinction, fossil, genes, reproduction, similar

What does the analogy describe or explain?

- I think that cars have changed through time because…

- I think that organisms change through time because…

- Changes to cars are decided by…

- The time-scale for changes to cars is…

- The time-scale for changes to organisms is…

- 'Survival of the fittest' would be represented in the analogy by…

What are the limitations of the analogy?

- I think that using cars through history as an analogy for natural selection is good because…

- I think that using cars through history as an analogy for natural selection is not good because…

How could the analogy be improved?

- I would adapt the analogy to make it better by…

- I think a better analogy would be…

NATIONAL CURRICULUM LINK

THE PARTICULATE NATURE OF MATTER

- the properties of the different states of matter (solid, liquid and gas) in terms of the particle model, including gas pressure
- changes of state in terms of the particle model

GUIDANCE ON THE MODEL

Bricks could be used to demonstrate this model to students. Student interpretation of the model can vary and still be correct. However, as a general guide, the bricks would represent particles within solids, liquids and gases. When stacked, they have a regular arrangement and are in fixed positions. When in the box, they are in an irregular pattern and can be moved around easily, whilst still remaining in contact with other particles and part of the whole group of particles. The bricks being thrown are separate from the group and are moving fast. Students should identify flaws with this model. For example, the bricks are not a good way to represent particles as they have no energy; the bricks do not vibrate within their fixed positions in the solid model; the bricks being thrown would immediately fall back to the ground; the particles in the box would not necessarily fill the container they are in, as some may stack on one another, unlike liquids; and the bricks representing a liquid would not flow easily.

Please refer to the generic guidance on pp 7–8 on how to use the following ACE Learning Ladder.

ACE LEARNING LADDER

Performance	Students may:
Advanced	• Explain in detail how the toy bricks model explains the particle model for solids liquids and gases. • Explain the limitations of the toy bricks model compared to the particle model for solids, liquids and gases. • Explain how the model could be improved or suggest and explain your own model for the particle model of solids, liquids and gases.
Confident	• Describe how the toy bricks model represents the particle model for solids, liquids and gases. • Describe the differences between the toy brick model and the particle model for solids, liquids and gases. • Describe how the model could be improved.
Establishing	• Match the parts of the toy bricks model to the key parts of the particle model for solids, liquids and gases. • State one problem with the model. • State how the model can be improved.

I think my brother's building bricks are like solids, liquids and gases. When he stacks them neatly they are like a solid, in the box they are like a liquid and when he throws them they are like a gas.
Do you agree?

POSSIBLE KEYWORDS TO USE:

arrangement, contact, different, energy, gas, irregular, liquid, material, particle, regular, similar, solid, still

SCIENTIFIC CONCEPTS THROUGH MODELS AND ANALOGIES: STIMULUS SHEET

What does the model describe or explain?

- I think the bricks represent…

- The stacked bricks are like a solid because…

- The bricks in the box are like a liquid because…

- The bricks in the air are like a gas because…

What are the limitations of the model?

- The bricks can only move if the child picks them up. In solids, liquids and gases…

- The stacked bricks are/are not a good way to represent a solid because…

- The bricks in the box are/are not a good way to represent a liquid because…

- The bricks being thrown in the air are/are not a good way to represent a gas because…

- I would adapt this model to represent changes of state (boiling, evaporating, condensing, freezing) by…

How could the model be improved?

- I think the model could be improved by…

- I think a better model would be…

NATIONAL CURRICULUM LINK

CHEMICAL REACTIONS

- chemical reactions as the rearrangement of atoms
- representing chemical reactions using formulae and using equations
- combustion, thermal decomposition, oxidation and displacement reactions

GUIDANCE ON THE ANALOGY

Student interpretation of the analogy can vary and still be correct. However, as a general guide, dancers represent the atoms found within substances. The initial pairs would be the reactants and during the dance (the reaction) the atoms would rearrange into the new pairs, which represent the products. Some flaws with the analogy students may identify could include: the reactants are both pairs, not all reactants contain two atoms, some may contain many atoms or only one type of atom; the dancers are not permanently combined, unlike atoms in chemical substances; the dancers could change the routine to join with different partners, whereas chemical reactions will always stay the same; and chemical reactions will be accompanied by various signs, such as colour changes or temperature changes, the dancers would not demonstrate such changes.

Please refer to the generic guidance on pp 7–8 on how to use the following ACE Learning Ladder.

ACE LEARNING LADDER

Performance	Students may:
Advanced	• Explain in detail how the dance analogy explains what happens to atoms during chemical reactions. • Explain the limitations of the dance analogy compared to what happens to atoms during chemical reactions. • Explain how the analogy could be improved or suggest and explain your own analogy for what happens to atoms during chemical reactions.
Confident	• Describe how the dance analogy represents what happens to atoms during chemical reactions. • Describe the differences between the dance analogy and what happens to atoms during chemical reactions. • Describe how the analogy could be improved.
Establishing	• Match the parts of the dance analogy to the key parts or processes involved when atoms take place in chemical reactions. • State one problem with the analogy. • State how the analogy can be improved.

POSSIBLE KEYWORDS TO USE:

atoms, bonds, break, compounds, different, energy, links, make, partner, people, products, reactants, reaction, similar

What does the analogy describe or explain?

- I think that the dancers represent…

- I think that the couples represent…

- I think that the dance routine represents…

- The reactants would be the…

- The products would be the…

What are the limitations of the analogy?

- I think that this is a good analogy for a chemical reaction because…

- I think that this is not a good analogy for a chemical reaction because…

How could the analogy be improved?

- The analogy could be improved by…

- I think a better analogy for a chemical reaction would be…

45

NATIONAL CURRICULUM LINK

ATOMS, ELEMENTS AND COMPOUNDS

• conservation of mass changes of state and chemical reactions

GUIDANCE ON THE ANALOGY

Student interpretation of the analogy can vary and still be correct. However, as a general guide, the mass of the luggage bag being taken onto the plane represents the mass of all atoms involved in a chemical reaction. The reactants in a chemical reaction would be represented by the bag initially placed in the luggage compartment. The products would be the luggage bag in its final arrangement. The 'reaction' is represented as the time the luggage is on the flight. For example, a bag could be placed in the luggage compartment containing many items that are then removed from the bag during the flight. The important point is that the total mass of the luggage items would not have changed during the flight (as there is no way for anything to be lost or gained) but the arrangement of the items could be different. Flaws in the analogy could include: people may eat or drink items from their luggage, in which case mass would appear to be lost; and items are not changing during the flight, merely changing location, whereas in a chemical reaction the atoms will rearrange through chemical reactions and so the reactants and products would be different from one another.

Please refer to the generic guidance on pp 7–8 on how to use the following ACE Learning Ladder.

ACE LEARNING LADDER

Performance	Students may:
Advanced	• Explain in detail how the analogy explains the conservation of mass. • Explain the limitations of the plane luggage analogy compared to the conservation of mass. • Explain how the analogy could be improved or suggest and explain your own analogy for the conservation of mass.
Confident	• Describe how the analogy represents the conservation of mass. • Describe the differences between the analogy and the conservation of mass. • Describe how the analogy could be improved.
Establishing	• Match the parts of the plane luggage analogy to the main parts or processes involved in the conservation of mass. • State one problem with the analogy. • State how the analogy can be improved.

When passengers go on a plane, all their luggage has to be weighed. Bags have to be put into the special cupboards above the seat when the plane takes off.

During the flight people usually get their luggage bag down, take things out of their bags, and may pass things between their friends and family. At the end of the flight, people will take all their luggage off the plane.

Is a luggage bag on a plane a good analogy for the conservation of mass during a chemical reaction?

POSSIBLE KEYWORDS TO USE:

atom, bond, closed, compound, different, finish, gain, loss, mass, position, products, reactants, reaction, similar, start

What does the analogy describe or explain?

- I think that the luggage bag on a plane would represent…

- I think that the time people are on the plane would represent…

- I think that reactants and products could be represented by…

What are the limitations of the analogy?

- It is important that the mass of the luggage is part of the analogy because…

- I think that the actual mass of the plane would/would not be like the conservation of mass because…

- The things that make it a good analogy for the conservation of mass are…

- The things that make it a bad analogy for the conservation of mass are…

How could the analogy be improved?

- I would improve the analogy by…

- I think a better analogy for the conservation of mass would be…

CHEMISTRY 4: TEACHER'S NOTES
DISSOLVING

NATIONAL CURRICULUM LINKS

PURE AND IMPURE SUBSTANCES

- the concept of a pure substance
- mixtures, including dissolving

THE PARTICULATE NATURE OF MATTER

- the properties of the different states of matter (solid, liquid and gas) in terms of the particle model, including gas pressure

ATOMS, ELEMENTS AND COMPOUNDS

- conservation of mass changes of state and chemical reactions

GUIDANCE ON THE MODEL

If possible, this model should be demonstrated to students before using this task. Student interpretation of the model can vary and still be correct. However, as a general guide, the dried peas in the glass jar represent solvent particles, with the sand representing solute particles. The solute is able to dissolve into the solvent and fill the tiny spaces in between the molecules. The mixture of sand and dried peas represents the final solution containing the dissolved substance. Students should identify flaws within the model. For example, both the sand and dried peas are in the solid phase, most dissolving involves a liquid solvent and a solid or liquid solute; the sand can still be seen in the final mixture in the jar, whereas many dissolved solutes will disappear, e.g. salt dissolved in water, although many will give a coloured solution; and some students may mention that there are interactions between solute particles and solvents that aid dissolution, but the model cannot show this.

Please refer to the generic guidance on pp 7–8 on how to use the following ACE Learning Ladder.

ACE LEARNING LADDER

Performance	Students may:
Advanced	• Explain in detail how the sand and dried peas model explains dissolving. • Explain the limitations of the model compared to the process of dissolving. • Explain how the model could be improved or suggest and explain your own model for dissolving.
Confident	• Describe how the sand and dried peas model represents dissolving. • Describe the differences between the model and dissolving. • Describe how the model could be improved.
Establishing	• Match the parts of the sand and dried peas model to the key parts and processes involved in dissolving. • State one problem with the model. • State how the model can be improved.

If a jar is filled with dried peas, it seems as though there is no space for anything else.

However, there is still plenty of room to add sand.

Is this a good model for explaining dissolving?

POSSIBLE KEYWORDS TO USE:

attraction, different, disappear, similar, size, solute, solution, solvent, space, spaces, visible

What does the model describe or explain?

- I think that the dried peas represent…

- I think that the sand represents…

- I think the mixture of sand and peas in the jar represents…

What are the limitations of the model?

- The sand can fit in the jar because…

- Substances can dissolve because…

- This is a good model for dissolving because…

- This is not a good model for dissolving because…

How could the model be improved?

- I would improve the model by…

- I think a better model for dissolving would be…

NATIONAL CURRICULUM LINK

CHEMICAL REACTIONS

- what catalysts do

GUIDANCE ON THE ANALOGY

Student interpretation of the analogy can vary and still be correct. However, as a general guide, the people completing the assault course represent particles taking part in a reaction. The time it takes for people to complete the assault course would be the reaction time (reaction rate), this would be sped up by the use of a catalyst. The staff member helping people over the assault course is like a catalyst as they remain unchanged at the end of the reaction and help the reaction happen more quickly. Students may suggest flaws including, some catalysts may be involved during reactions but remain unchanged afterwards whereas the staff member shown does not; the people doing the assault course are not changing during the course, unlike reactants; and the people doing the assault course would complete the course at different rates, whereas reactions have one overall rate of reaction (in terms of the reaction being complete – no consideration of initial rates is needed at this level).

Please refer to the generic guidance on pp 7–8 on how to use the following ACE Learning Ladder.

ACE LEARNING LADDER

Performance	Students may:
Advanced	• Explain in detail how the assault course helper analogy explains catalysts. • Explain the limitations of the assault course helper analogy compared to the actual workings of a catalyst. • Explain how the analogy could be improved or suggest and explain your own analogy for catalysts.
Confident	• Describe how the assault course helper analogy represents catalysts. • Describe the differences between the analogy and the actual workings of a catalyst. • Describe how the analogy could be improved.
Establishing	• Match the parts of the assault course helper analogy to the key parts or processes involved when a catalyst is used to speed up a reaction. • State one problem with the analogy. • State how the analogy can be improved.

POSSIBLE KEYWORDS TO USE:

atoms, bonds, catalyst, change, compounds, different, energy, finish, people, reaction, rearrange, similar, start

What does the analogy describe or explain?

• I think that the assault course is like…

• I think that the people doing the assault course are like…

• The time people take to complete the assault course is like…

What are the limitations of the analogy?

• The person helping is like a catalyst because…

• The person helping is not like a catalyst because…

• I think it is important that the person helping doesn't do the assault course because…

How could the analogy be improved?

• Different reactions have different catalysts. I could adapt the analogy to show this by…

• I could improve this analogy by…

• I think a better analogy for a catalyst would be…

NATIONAL CURRICULUM LINK

MATERIALS

- the order of metals and carbon in the reactivity series
- the use of carbon in obtaining metals from metal oxides

GUIDANCE ON THE ANALOGY

Student interpretation of the analogy can vary and still be correct. However, as a general guide, the boxers each represent a different metal found in the reactivity series. Each person's skill at boxing represents their reactivity and a fight between two boxers represents a reaction between two metals (see comment later about metal compounds). In the analogy, Pascal is said to beat everyone, so this would mean he was a very reactive metal such as magnesium, found near the top of the reactivity series. Will is always beaten by everyone, meaning he represents a highly unreactive metal found at the bottom of the reactivity series, such as gold or silver. One major flaw with the analogy shown is that the boxers would compete as individuals, whereas in chemical reactions that illustrate reactivity, the less reactive metal is usually found within a compound prior to the displacement reaction (the more reactive compound can also come from a compound), from which it becomes displaced.

Please refer to the generic guidance on pp 7–8 on how to use the following ACE Learning Ladder.

ACE LEARNING LADDER

Performance	Students may:
Advanced	• Explain in detail how the boxers analogy explains the reactivity of metals. • Explain the limitations of the analogy compared to the reactivity of metals. • Explain how the analogy could be improved or suggest and explain your own analogy for the reactivity of metals.
Confident	• Describe how the boxers analogy represents the reactivity of metals. • Describe the differences between the analogy and the reactivity of metals. • Describe how the analogy could be improved.
Establishing	• Match the parts of the boxers analogy to the parts or processes relevant to the reactivity of metals. • State one problem with the analogy. • State how the analogy can be improved.

POSSIBLE KEYWORDS TO USE:

better, compound, different, displace, element, metal, power, reactivity, similar, strength

What does the analogy describe or explain?

- I think the boxers represent…

- I think how good each one is at boxing is similar to…

- A fight between two boxers represents…

- Who wins in a fight represents what would happen in…

What are the limitations of the analogy?

- Non-metals, like carbon, are included in the reactivity series. This could be part of the analogy by…

- I think that this is a good way of representing the reactivity series of metals because…

- I think that this is not a good way of representing the reactivity series of metals because…

How could the analogy be improved?

- I would adapt the analogy to make it better by…

- I think a better analogy would be…

2 CHEMISTRY 7: TEACHER'S NOTES
THE STRUCTURE OF THE EARTH

NATIONAL CURRICULUM LINK

EARTH AND ATMOSPHERE

- the composition of the Earth
- the structure of the Earth
- the carbon cycle

GUIDANCE ON THE MODEL

Student interpretation of the model can vary and still be correct. However, as a general guide, the breadcrumbs of the Scotch egg would represent the Earth's crust, the sausage meat would represent the mantle, the egg white would represent the outer core and the egg yolk would represent the inner core. The egg has the same number of layers as the Earth, but these layers are not representative of the relative size of the layers within the Earth, although the breadcrumbs are a very small relative thickness, as is the Earth's crust. The layers within the egg are all static and all solid, whereas the crust is in constant movement due to tectonic plate movement, due to currents within the mantle and parts of the core are able to move, and only the crust and inner core are considered solid. The Earth is almost spherical, whereas an egg is not.

Please refer to the generic guidance on pp 7–8 on how to use the following ACE Learning Ladder.

ACE LEARNING LADDER

Performance	Students may:
Advanced	• Explain in detail how the model explains the structure of the Earth. • Explain the limitations of the model compared to the structure of the Earth. • Explain how the model could be improved or suggest and explain your own model for the structure of the Earth.
Confident	• Describe how the model represents the structure of the Earth. • Describe the differences between the scotch egg model and the structure of the Earth. • Describe how the model could be improved.
Establishing	• Match the parts of the scotch egg model to the structure of the Earth. • State one problem with the model. • State how the model can be improved.

Is a scotch egg a good model for the structure of the Earth?

POSSIBLE KEYWORDS TO USE:

breadcrumbs, core, crust, different, layer, liquid, magnetic, mantle, pressure, solid, similar, temperature, white, yolk

What does the model describe or explain?

- The inside of a scotch egg contains…

- The inside of the Earth contains

- The yolk would represent…

- The egg white would represent…

- The sausage meat would represent…

- The breadcrumbs would represent…

What are the limitations of the model?

- A scotch egg is similar to the Earth because…

- A scotch egg is not similar to the Earth because…

- A scotch egg would be more like the Earth if…

How could the model be improved?

- I would improve the model by…

- I think a better model for the structure of the Earth is…

NATIONAL CURRICULUM LINK

EARTH AND ATMOSPHERE

- the composition of the atmosphere
- the production of carbon dioxide by human activity and the impact on climate

GUIDANCE ON THE ANALOGY

Student interpretation of the analogy can vary and still be correct. However, as a general guide, the duvet represents CO_2 in the atmosphere. One duvet would keep the Earth at a comfortable temperature by trapping an adequate amount of radiation and allowing some to escape back out to space (the greenhouse effect). Adding more and more duvets represents excessive emissions of CO_2 into the atmosphere, which traps more and more radiation, and prevents the normal loss of radiation back into space. This would represent global warming. Once the duvets caused the Earth to actually change, in terms of climate, on a long-term basis, this would then represent climate change. Flaws in the analogy include the duvets being a fixed item, whereas carbon dioxide enters and leaves the atmosphere constantly via the carbon cycle; and the duvet appears homogenous, whereas the atmosphere contains many different substances, some of which are greenhouse gases, some of which are not. The analogy also does not allow for the influence of other possible factors that influence global warming such as sun spots.

Please refer to the generic guidance on pp 7–8 on how to use the following ACE Learning Ladder.

ACE LEARNING LADDER

Performance	Students may:
Advanced	• Explain in detail how the duvet analogy explains global warming. • Explain the limitations of the analogy compared to the actual process of global warming. • Explain how the model could be improved or suggest and explain your own model for global warming.
Confident	• Describe how the duvet analogy represents global warming. • Describe the differences between the duvet analogy and the process of global warming. • Describe how the analogy could be improved.
Establishing	• Match the parts of the duvet analogy to the key parts involved in global warming. • State one problem with the analogy. • State how the analogy can be improved.

Imagine we could wrap the Earth in a duvet and then add more and more duvets.

Would this be a good analogy for describing how adding more carbon dioxide to the atmosphere causes global warming?

POSSIBLE KEYWORDS TO USE:

absorb, atmosphere, carbon dioxide, climate, different, duvet, energy, greenhouse gases, insulate, material, similar, temperature, trap

What does the analogy describe or explain?

- The duvet around the Earth represents…

- Adding more duvets represents…

- The extra duvets make the Earth heat up. This is like adding more CO_2 to the atmosphere because…

What are the limitations of the analogy?

- The analogy could explain what the difference between the greenhouse effect and global warming is by…

- The analogy could be used to explain what climate change is by…

How could the analogy be improved?

- I think this is a good analogy for global warming because…

- I think this is not a good analogy for global warming because…

- I would improve the analogy by…

- I think a better analogy for global warming is…

PHYSICS 1: TEACHER'S NOTES
BROWNIAN MOTION

NATIONAL CURRICULUM LINK

PHYSICAL CHANGES

- Brownian motion in gases

GUIDANCE ON THE ANALOGY

Student interpretation of the analogy can vary and still be correct. However, as a general guide, the Year 7 students represent gaseous particles constantly moving in a random fashion. Students should identify flaws with the analogy. For example, their motion is not perfectly random as they would choose where to go, even if they were lost; they are only able to move along the ground, not in all directions, unlike gaseous particles; and if a student stood still, they would not appear to be continually moving, whereas particles constantly fluctuate in their movements.

Please refer to the generic guidance on pp 7–8 on how to use the following ACE Learning Ladder.

ACE LEARNING LADDER

Performance	Students may:
Advanced	• Explain in detail how the new students analogy explains Brownian motion. • Explain the limitations of the new students analogy compared to Brownian motion. • Explain how the analogy could be improved or suggest and explain your own analogy for Brownian motion.
Confident	• Describe how the new students analogy represents Brownian motion. • Describe the differences between the new students analogy and Brownian motion. • Describe how the analogy could be improved.
Establishing	• Match the parts of the new students analogy to the key parts or processes involved in Brownian motion. • State one problem with the analogy. • State how the analogy can be improved.

Scientific Concepts through Models and Analogies: Stimulus Sheet

What does the analogy describe or explain?

- I think the Year 7 students represent…

- If particles show Brownian motion they…

What are the limitations of the analogy?

- The movement of the students is like Brownian motion because…

- The movement of the students is not like Brownian motion because…

- I think this is a good analogy for Brownian motion because…

- I think this is not a good analogy for Brownian motion because…

How could the analogy be improved?

- I would adapt the analogy by…

- I think a better analogy would be…

NATIONAL CURRICULUM LINK

PHYSICAL CHANGES

- diffusion in liquids and gases driven by differences in concentration

GUIDANCE ON THE ANALOGY

Student interpretation of the analogy can vary and still be correct. However, as a general guide, the people getting into the pool represent any substance being placed into a liquid, and initially being in a high concentration. Over time, the people would spread out until they all have more space and no one particular area of the pool is more overcrowded than any other area. This represents diffusion occurring, driven by a concentration difference, with particles moving from a high concentration into a low concentration area. Students should identify flaws with the analogy. For example, people in the pool could all choose to gather in one area of the pool (for a particular game, for instance), whereas particles would not randomly be able to collect back into an area of high concentration; people in the pool may stay static in one location, whereas particles are constantly in motion; and people could get into the pool without using the steps.

Please refer to the generic guidance on pp 7–8 on how to use the following ACE Learning Ladder.

ACE LEARNING LADDER

Performance	Students may:
Advanced	• Explain in detail how the swimming pool analogy explains diffusion in a liquid. • Explain the limitations of the swimming pool analogy compared to diffusion in a liquid. • Explain how the analogy could be improved or suggest and explain your own analogy for diffusion in a liquid.
Confident	• Describe how the swimming pool analogy represents diffusion in a liquid. • Describe the differences between the swimming pool analogy and diffusion in a liquid. • Describe how the analogy could be improved.
Establishing	• Match the parts of the swimming pool analogy to the key parts or processes involved in diffusion in a liquid. • State one problem with the analogy. • State how the analogy can be improved.

There is only one set of steps into the pool. Everyone is at one end when the pool opens.

Eventually, they all spread out across the whole pool.

I think this is like diffusion in a liquid. Do you agree?

POSSIBLE KEYWORDS TO USE:

busy, concentration, different, empty, energy, equal, high, low, particles, similar

---

SCIENTIFIC CONCEPTS THROUGH MODELS AND ANALOGIES: **STIMULUS SHEET**

What does the analogy describe or explain?

- I think the people getting into the pool represent…

- I think the swimming pool and the water represent…

- Particles spread out when they diffuse because…

- When the people first get in the pool their concentration is…

- It is important that concentration is part of the analogy for diffusion because…

What are the limitations of the analogy?

- If some people got out of the pool, everyone else would…
  This is like/not like diffusion because…

- I could adapt the analogy to show what happens when gases diffuse by…

- I think this is a good analogy for diffusion because…

- I think this is not a good analogy for diffusion because…

How could the analogy be improved?

- I would adapt the analogy to improve it by…

- I think a better analogy for diffusion would be…

NATIONAL CURRICULUM LINK

CURRENT ELECTRICITY

- electric current, measured in amperes, in circuits, series and parallel circuits, currents add where branches meet and current as flow of charge
- potential difference, measured in volts, battery and bulb ratings; resistance, measured in ohms, as the ratio of potential difference (p.d.) to current

GUIDANCE ON THE ANALOGY

Student interpretation of the analogy can vary and still be correct. However, as a general guide, the riders could represent the electrons in a circuit, carrying packages which represent charge. The flow of riders around the streets is representing current. Series circuits could be shown by a single circular route, whereas parallel circuits could be shown by parallel roads. Flaws in the analogy include riders carrying different packages, as all electrons in a circuit are equivalent. Riders may travel in different directions and at different speeds whereas electrons will all flow in the same way. The depot that gives out the packages could be seen as representing the battery, when the depot is empty the battery is 'flat', as riders have nothing to deliver anymore.

Please refer to the generic guidance on pp 7–8 on how to use the following ACE Learning Ladder.

ACE LEARNING LADDER

Performance	Students may:
Advanced	• Explain in detail how the cycle courier analogy explains electrons in a circuit. • Explain the limitations of the cycle courier analogy compared to electrons in a circuit. • Explain how the analogy could be improved or suggest and explain your own analogy for electrons in a circuit.
Confident	• Describe how the cycle courier analogy represents electrons in a circuit. • Describe the differences between the analogy and electrons in a circuit. • Describe how the analogy could be improved.
Establishing	• Match the parts of the cycle courier analogy to the key parts or processes relating to electrons in a circuit. • State one problem with the analogy. • State how the analogy can be improved.

POSSIBLE KEYWORDS TO USE:

amps, battery, charge, current, different, electron, energy, parcel, route, similar, speed, voltage

What does the analogy describe or explain?

- I think the riders represent…

- The riders' parcels and packages could represent…

- 'Current' would be like…

What are the limitations of the analogy?

- The riders will stop work and go home at the end of the day. This is similar/not similar to electrons because…

- Riders may choose different roads to cycle on. Electrons in a circuit…

- This analogy could represent a battery by …

- I would adapt this analogy to represent series and parallel circuits by…

- I think the analogy could explain what voltage is by…

How could the analogy be improved?

- I would adapt the analogy to improve it by…

- I think a better analogy for electrons in a circuit would be…

NATIONAL CURRICULUM LINK

CURRENT ELECTRICITY

- potential difference, measured in volts, battery and bulb ratings; resistance, measured in ohms, as the ratio of potential difference (p.d.) to current
- differences in resistance between conducting and insulating components (quantitative)

GUIDANCE ON THE ANALOGY

Student interpretation of the analogy can vary and still be correct. However, as a general guide, the passengers travelling through the station represent electrons traveling through a wire. The ticket barriers represent the atoms of the material that electrons collide with during their movement through the wire. Insulating materials have high resistance, which would be represented by a high number of ticket barriers. Students should identify flaws in the analogy. For example, the passengers do not have to travel in the same direction; the station would not heat up due to passengers passing through the ticket barriers, whereas resistance in wires causes a temperature increase; the analogy does not show any significant changes in the passengers before and after passing through the barriers so does not adequately cover changes in potential difference; and the arrangement of the barriers is infrequent but regular, whereas atoms that electrons encounter will be arranged more regularly and not necessarily in a set pattern.

Please refer to the generic guidance on pp 7–8 on how to use the following ACE Learning Ladder.

ACE LEARNING LADDER

Performance	Students may:
Advanced	• Explain in detail how the ticket barrier analogy explains resistance in insulators. • Explain the limitations of the analogy compared to the resistance in insulators. • Explain how the analogy could be improved or suggest and explain your own analogy for resistance in insulators.
Confident	• Describe how the ticket barrier analogy represents resistance in insulators. • Describe the differences between the analogy and resistance in insulators. • Describe how the analogy could be improved.
Establishing	• Match the parts of the ticket barrier analogy to the key parts and processes involved in resistance in insulators. • State one problem with the analogy. • State how the analogy can be improved.

3 RESISTANCE IN INSULATORS

Passengers using train stations have to pass through ticket barriers.

Barriers often make it harder for passengers to move through the station.

Is this a good analogy to explain resistance in insulating materials?

POSSIBLE KEYWORDS TO USE:

atoms, different, direction, electrons, energy, particles, people, resistance, similar, temperature, tickets

SCIENTIFIC CONCEPTS THROUGH MODELS AND ANALOGIES: STIMULUS SHEET

What does the analogy describe or explain?

- I think the passengers represent…

- I think the train station represents…

- I think the barriers represent…

- When passengers go through barriers I think this is like…

- Resistance is…

What are the limitations of the analogy?

- The resistance of an insulator is high/low. This means that …

- The resistance of a conductor is high/low. This means that…

- Potential difference is related to resistance. The analogy could show this by…

- I would adapt this analogy to represent conducting materials by…

- I think this is a good analogy for resistance in insulating materials because…

- I think this is not a good analogy for resistance in insulating materials because…

How could the analogy be improved?

- I would adapt the analogy by…

- I think a better analogy would be…

3 PHYSICS 5: TEACHER'S NOTES
ENERGY CARRIED BY WAVES

NATIONAL CURRICULUM LINK

ENERGY AND WAVES

- pressure waves transferring energy; use for cleaning and physiotherapy by ultra-sound; waves transferring information for conversion to electrical signals by microphone

GUIDANCE ON THE ANALOGY

Student interpretation of the analogy can vary and still be correct. However, as a general guide, the waves in the water represent any oscillation to form a wave such as in water or air. The rubber duck on the water represents the energy being carried by the wave. It is being transferred, but the actual water is not moving significantly. The baby making the waves initially represents any action that causes a wave to be started, such as banging a drum causes a sound wave to begin. Bigger and smaller waves in the bath would represent bigger and smaller amplitudes of waves. Students should identify flaws in the analogy. For example, the water in the bath will move slightly, perhaps some will spill out of the bath; the waves being represented are transverse, the analogy does not cover longitudinal waves; and due to the small space in a bath, waves may cancel out, reflect or add to each other, this may cause the rubber duck not to move along the bath, whereas the energy transfer in a real wave would not just stop in these instances.

Please refer to the generic guidance on pp 7–8 on how to use the following ACE Learning Ladder.

ACE LEARNING LADDER

Performance	Students may:
Advanced	• Explain in detail how the rubber duck analogy explains energy being carried by a wave. • Explain the limitations of the rubber duck analogy compared to the energy being carried by a wave. • Explain how the analogy could be improved or suggest and explain your own analogy for energy being carried by a wave.
Confident	• Describe how the rubber duck analogy represents energy being carried by a wave. • Describe the differences between the rubber duck analogy and energy being carried by a wave. • Describe how the analogy could be improved.
Establishing	• Match the parts of the rubber duck analogy to the key parts or processes involved in energy being carried by a wave. • State one problem with the analogy. • State how the analogy can be improved.

POSSIBLE KEYWORDS TO USE:

amplitude, different, displace, energy, frequency, gases, height, liquids, object, particles, similar, solids, speed

What does the analogy describe or explain?

- I think the rubber duck represents…

- I think the moving water represents…

- I think the baby making waves in the water represents…

What are the limitations of the analogy?

- Water in the bath stays where it is (it doesn't end up at one end of the bath) when waves are made. This is important because…

- Bigger waves would mean…

- Smaller waves would mean…

- A rubber duck in a bath is a good analogy for energy being carried along by waves because…

- A rubber duck in a bath is not a good analogy for energy being carried along by waves because…

How could the analogy be improved?

- I would improve the analogy by…

- I think a better analogy for energy being carried by waves would be…

National Curriculum Link

Light waves

• colours and the different frequencies of light, white light and prisms (qualitative only); differential colour effects in absorption and diffuse reflection

Guidance on the Analogy

Student interpretation of the analogy can vary and still be correct. However, as a general guide, paint arriving as a delivery is all contained together and the individual parts cannot be seen, hence, it is representing white light. When it has been unpacked and separated into its components, it has become individual colours of paint, and so representing the individual coloured components of light. The person unpacking the paint is causing the colours to be separated and, therefore, represents the prism. Students should be able to identify several flaws with the analogy. For example, the components of the light do not possess any characteristic that distinguishes them other than observed colour, unlike in light where the colours have different frequencies; the person separating the paint is physically separating the colours and moving them, whereas light is dispersed but the colours are not completely separated out from one another; and the analogy cannot take account of the diffraction through the prism.

Please refer to the generic guidance on pp 7–8 on how to use the following ACE Learning Ladder.

ACE LEARNING LADDER

Performance	Students may:
Advanced	• Explain in detail how the paint delivery analogy explains the effect prisms have on light. • Explain the limitations of the paint delivery analogy compared to the effect prisms have on light. • Explain how the analogy could be improved or suggest and explain your own analogy for light through a prism.
Confident	• Describe how the paint delivery analogy represents the effect prisms have on light. • Describe the differences between the paint delivery analogy and effect prisms have on light. • Describe how the analogy could be improved.
Establishing	• Match the parts of the paint delivery analogy to the key parts or processes involved when light passes through a prism. • State one problem with the analogy. • State how the analogy can be improved.

What does the analogy describe or explain?

- I think the paint arriving in the delivery represents…

- I think the paint on the shelves represents…

- I think the person working in the paint shop thinks they are like a prism because…

What are the limitations of the analogy?

- Light is made up of…

- The paint delivery is made up of…

- A delivery of paint being separated into colours is a good analogy for a prism because…

- A delivery of paint being separated into colours is not a good analogy for a prism because…

How could the analogy be improved?

- I would improve the analogy by…

- I think a better analogy for light passing through a prism would be…

PHYSICS 7: TEACHER'S NOTES
COLOUR FILTERS

NATIONAL CURRICULUM LINK

LIGHT WAVES

- colours and the different frequencies of light, white light and prisms (qualitative only); differential colour effects in absorption and diffuse reflection

GUIDANCE ON THE ANALOGY

Student interpretation of the analogy can vary and still be correct. However, as a general guide, the guests waiting to go into the party represent white light. The door staff represent a green filter in this instance, as they only allow guests wearing green to go in, meaning that the guests who have gained entry to the party would represent green light. The analogy could be adapted to represent different colours of light by the door staff allowing other colours to pass through, e.g. only guests wearing blue if they were representing a blue filter. Students should be able to identify flaws in the analogy. For example, the guests queuing up are not combined so that their clothing colour cannot be seen, whereas the relevant parts of white light are not visible until after they have passed through the filter; the guests only pass the door staff in the analogy, white light has to pass through a filter; and filters would heat up marginally when light is passing through them, this would not occur in the analogy.

Please refer to the generic guidance on pp 7–8 on how to use the following ACE Learning Ladder.

ACE LEARNING LADDER

Performance	Students may:
Advanced	• Explain in detail how the clothing colour analogy explains filters. • Explain the limitations of the clothing colour analogy compared to filters. • Explain how the analogy could be improved or suggest and explain your own analogy for filters.
Confident	• Describe how the clothing colour analogy represents filters. • Describe the differences between the analogy and filters. • Describe how the analogy could be improved.
Establishing	• Match the parts of the clothing colours analogy to the key parts or processes relating to filters. • State one problem with the analogy. • State how the analogy can be improved.

What does the analogy describe or explain?

- I think the guests queuing up represent…

- I think the door staff represent a …

- I think that the guests who have been allowed into the party represent…

- Filters work by…

- I think the type of filter represented in this analogy is…

What are the limitations of the analogy?

- There are lots of different colour filters. The analogy could represent a purple filter by…   or other colour filters by…

- The analogy could show what happens when more than one filter is used by…

- Party guests only being allowed in if they are wearing certain colours is a good analogy for a filter because…

- Party guests only being allowed in if they are wearing certain colours is not a good analogy because…

How could the analogy be improved?

- I would improve the analogy by…

- I think a better analogy for a filter would be…